Nibble Mania ®

by

Cathy Prange

and

Joan Pauli

Published and Distributed by
Muffin Mania Publishing Co.,
553 Greenbrook Drive,
Kitchener, Ontario.   N2M 4K5

Printed by Ainsworth Press
Kitchener, Ontario

Sketches by Miriam Stanbury

I.S.B.N.   0-9691485-4-2

Nibble Mania

Many Friday mornings have come and gone through our kitchens since Muffin Mania first hit the book shelves -- and yes, we are still baking those scrumptious muffins. However, not quite as often as before, as our families are quick to point out. As a matter of fact, we've been forced to alter our daily cooking pattern in order to respond to the tremendous support you have given us for Muffin Mania.

Many were the nights that the meals consisted of finger food, simple snacks, appetizers, or whatever you want to call them, and before we knew it, we found ourselves right in the middle of a brand new craze, or mania, which we now want to share with you. As you'll find out, Nibble Mania can be as much fun as Muffin Mania!

Nibbles are so simple and so easy to make. They're scrumptious and nutritious to eat -- our families and nibble-tasting gal friends can vouch for that! Once again we called upon their taste buds and endorsements to be sure we offered you only the best recipes. Their encouragement has convinced us to share our very favourite, well-tested recipes with you.

You don't have to put away your muffin tins! They can be used for several of our recipes. These easy nibbles can be made ahead, frozen, and heated as needed at a later date -- ideal if friends drop in for dinner, lunch, a party or just a drink. It's nice to be prepared and you'll be an instant hit! They are also great for a quiet evening at home or at the cottage in front of a candle or the fireplace.

So gals, and all you guys who love to cook, we're sure you'll find a nifty nibble to suit almost any occasion and the best part is, you can relax and enjoy too!

Have fun and good tasting!

Sisters, Partners, and Yes,

Still Friends,

Cathy Prange

Joan Pauli

Hints

Have everything ready,
Before guests are due.
You'll enjoy yourself more,
And they will too!

1. When serving these as an appeteaser before dinner, limit them to four kinds as they should stimulate the appetite rather than satisfy.

2. Whichever you choose to serve, keep your tray simple and uncluttered. Have interesting combinations as to colour and taste.

3. If freezing and reheating, wrap in foil to prevent drying. Bake at 300° for 10 min. if thawed, or until hot.

4. Those made in muffin cups may be served for lunch by using larger tins and not separating biscuits. The fillings may also be put into toast cups, bouchées made with puff pastry or tart shells.

5. Cheese balls may be kept for several days in the refrigerator. Freeze for longer storage. To freeze cheese balls, wrap in plastic wrap or foil and thaw in refrigerator.

6. For easy unmolding of mousses, grease mold first and put in freezer while preparing the filling.

7. For variety and time-saving, get together with friends and exchange your nifty nibbles.

Table Of Contents

Table of contents continued:

Say Cheese

Table of contents continued:

Dips and Spreads

Table of contents continued:

Hooked On Sea Food

NIBBLES

Celery Seed Bread

1 loaf French bread unsliced
1/2 c. butter softened
1 tsp. celery or poppy seed
1/4 tsp. salt
1/4 tsp. paprika
dash cayenne

Slice bread lengthwise nearly to bottom and then across in 1 inch sections.

Mix all ingredients and spread mixture in and out of every slice and ice the top with left over.

Place buttered loaf on baking sheet.

Cover with waxed paper and chill.

Uncover and bake 400° for 15 - 20 min. until golden.

To make spreading easier, melt butter and add seasonings and brush the sections. We sometimes double the mixture so we have lots to ice the top.

This will bring raves and is a nice change from garlic bread.

Cheese Snacks

1 c. sharp cheddar cheese grated
1 c. crushed potato chips
1/4 c. soft butter
1/2 c. flour
1 tsp. prepared mustard

Blend all ingredients and drop from teaspoon on ungreased cookie sheet.

Flatten with the back of a spoon and bake at 375° for 5 - 8 min.

Store in tins. Keep in refrigerator.

May be frozen.

These are a delicious nibble served hot or cold.

Cheese Wafers

1 pkg. Imperial cheese softened (the
  kind in the flat round container)
1/2 c. corn oil
3 tsp. worcestershire sauce
  dash cayenne red pepper
1 c. flour
2 c. Rice Krispies

Mix together cheese, oil, flour, worcestershire and cayenne.

Stir in Rice Krispies.

Form into small balls. Place on cookie
sheet and flatten with a fork which has
been dipped into cold water.

Bake 325° for 10 - 12 min. or until
golden. Store in tins in refrigerator.

May be frozen.

These are good served hot or cold.

Why not add 1/2 c. crumbled bacon or
bacon bits to these? M-m-m good!

3

Helen's Cheese Short Bread

2 c. grated sharp cheese
1 c. soft butter
2 c. flour
1 tsp. salt

Cream butter and cheese. Mix in flour and salt. Chill.

Cut in shapes and bake 12 min. at 350° or until slightly browned.

OR

Mold into two rolls, 1" in diameter. (Dough may be soft, but not to worry!)

Wrap in wax paper and refrigerate two hours or over night.

Cut into 1/4" slices and bake as above.

Serve hot!

Delicious any time of the day — or night.

Nuts and Bolts

1 lb. salted mixed nuts
1/2 lb. cashews
1/2 lb. peanuts
1 box Shreddies
1 box Cheerios
1 pkg. (8 oz.) pretzel sticks, cut in half
2 c. peanut oil or 1 c. butter and 1 c. peanut oil
2 tbsp. worcestershire sauce
1 tbsp. garlic salt
1 tbsp. seasoned salt
1 tsp. celery salt

In large roasting pan, combine first six ingredients.

Mix remaining ingredients together and pour over mixture in pan.

Bake 200° for 2 hrs. Stir frequently.

Pack into jars. This may be frozen in freezer bags.

This makes a very large quantity so it may easily be cut in half.

Nice to pack in jars as gifts at Christmas time.

Oriental Munch

1/2 c. butter
4 tbsp. soya sauce
2 tsp. seasoned salt
2 tsp. worcestershire sauce
1 tsp. tabasco sauce
1/2 tsp. garlic powder
2 c. chow mein noodles
2 c. pretzel sticks halved
2 c. Shreddies
2 c. Riceroos
1 c. pecans
1 c. cashews

Melt butter and stir in the next five ingredients (seasonings).

Place remaining ingredients in roasting pan and pour butter mixture over. Toss lightly to blend.

Place in oven at 200° for 1 hr., stirring occasionally.

Pack into jars. "Yummy."

If you can't find Riceroos, Rice Chex or Cheerios may be substituted.

A great nibble for your bridge table, but have the drinks ready!

Spicy Breadsticks

1/2 c. butter
1/2 tsp. garlic salt
1/2 tsp. celery salt
1/2 tsp. seasoned salt
1 1/2 tbsp. worcestershire
2 dashes tabasco
2 pkg. Bread Sticks

Heat oven 300°.

Put butter in roasting pan and heat until melted. Remove and stir in seasoning.

Roll sticks until coated on all sides. Spread out on cookie sheet and heat 20 min.

Turn several times then turn oven off and leave in until crispy and dry.

Will keep in covered tin.

A fun finger food to serve with soups, salads and dips.

7

Auntie Thelma's Almond Toffee

3/4 c. butter

Melt over low heat.

Add 1 c. white sugar (she uses 3/4 c.)
Stir gently and just before it boils
add 1 c. whole unblanched almonds.

Boil moderately (stirring) until real
hard when tested in cold water, about
10 - 15 min.

Pour quickly over an ungreased cookie
sheet spreading almonds evenly.

Spread scant layer of chocolate chips
on top of toffee and let melt.

Spread carefully over toffee.

Sprinkle 1/3 c. of crushed pecans on
top.

Put in refrigerator until hard.

Break into small pieces with fingers
and place in refrigerator in a tin.

Without a doubt, the best candy our
families have ever tasted! Our Christmas
would not be complete without receiving
our box from Auntie Thelma.

Candied Nuts

2 c. peanuts (without skins)
1/2 c. sugar
2 tbsp. butter
1 tsp. vanilla
3/4 tsp. salt

In large frypan, heat nuts, sugar and butter over medium heat stirring constantly until golden brown — about 15 min.

Remove from heat and stir in vanilla.

Spread mixture on lightly buttered cookie sheet. Sprinkle with salt. Cool and break into clusters.

If salted peanuts are used, omit salt.

These are especially good when whole unblanched almonds are used.

Pack these marvelous munchies in pretty jars to give to friends before your family tastes them!

Chocolate Clusters

1 6 oz. pkg. chocolate chips
1 6 oz. pkg. butterscotch chips

Melt together and add:

1 c. chow mein noodles
1 c. peanuts

Drop by teaspoon on waxed paper and cool.

Store in tins in refrigerator.

Cornflake Nibblers

2 pkgs. (6 oz. each) butterscotch chips
1/2 c. peanut butter
6 c. cornflakes

Melt chips and peanut butter together in large saucepan over low heat.

Add cornflakes and mix well.

Drop by large teaspoon on waxed paper.

Refrigerate for several hours.

Put in tin and store in refrigerator.

Both these recipes may be frozen in plastic bags. A colourful addition to your Christmas cookie tray.

HOT STUFF

Blue Cheese Bites

1 pkg. refrigerator biscuits

Cut each biscuit in quarters and arrange in a baking dish.

Melt: 1/4 c. butter
        4 oz. blue cheese

Pour over biscuits coating well.
Bake 12 - 15 min. at 400°.   Makes 40.

These would be delicious using cheddar or any kind of cheese.

What could be easier than this quick appeteaser for the working gal or guy?

11

Cocktail Meat Balls In Barbeque Sauce

2 lbs. ground lean beef
1 egg
1 pkg. onion soup mix (dry)
2 tsp. accent
1/4 c. bread crumbs

Mix together and form into 1" balls and brown.

Barbeque Sauce

1 pkg. spaghetti sauce mix (dry)
2 small jars red currant jelly
2 small bottles ketchup

Put all in saucepan and simmer 40 min.

Add meatballs and heat through. Serve with cocktail picks.

Meatballs may be frozen in plastic bags after browning and added to sauce when needed.

Eat sparingly - almost a meal in itself!

Cocktail Weiners

Mix 1 6 oz. jar of prepared mustard and 1 10 oz. jar of red currant jelly in a saucepan over low heat.

Slice 1 lb. (8 - 10 frankfurters) diagonally into bite-size pieces.

Add to sauce and heat through. Serve hot with picks.

Joye's Sausage & Cheese Balls

1 lb. sausage meat
2 c. tea-bisk
10 oz. sharp cheddar cheese grated

Mix ingredients with hands and roll into 1" balls.

Bake 325° for 30 min. or until slightly brown.

May be frozen, unbaked on cookie sheet and store in plastic bag until ready to use. Bake from frozen state. Serve hot.

Good when dipped in all our homemade sauces.

Duncan's Chicken Wings (Sweet & Sour)

2 lbs. chicken wings
2 tbsp. wine vinegar
4 tbsp. oil
2 tbsp. soya sauce
2 large garlic cloves crushed
2 tbsp. orange marmalade
2 tbsp. honey
1 tbsp. lemon juice

Wash chicken wings, cut in half at joint and discard tips.

Combine ingredients in a large baking dish.

Place wings in dish, turning well to coat each wing and allow to marinate for one hour or more, turning several times to coat.

Bake uncovered in 350° oven for approx. 1 hour, turning wings occasionally to baste.

These wings are delicious hot or cold, or served with blue cheese dressing.
(See page 41)

Hot Spinach Balls

2 pkg. (10 oz. each) frozen spinach, cooked and drained very well
2 c. packaged stuffing mix
1 c. grated parmesan cheese
6 eggs beaten
3/4 c. softened butter
1 tbsp. garlic salt
1/2 tsp. accent
1/2 tsp. pepper
1/2 tsp. thyme

Combine all ingredients, mixing well.

Roll into balls about the size of a walnut. Put on cookie sheet and freeze. When frozen, put in freezer bags.

Bake from frozen state 10 - 15 min. at 350°.

These are quite gooey when rolling into balls so don't fret.

They are moist and delicious for those who like spinach.

Julia's Cheese Things

1 pkg. refrigerator crescent rolls
4 tbsp. butter
3 eggs beaten
1 c. broken salad olives
1 onion chopped
4 c. grated sharp cheddar cheese
dash cayenne pepper

Unwrap crescent rolls and pat into
9 X 15 pan, smoothing out the seams.

Mix all the ingredients and pour over
dough.

Bake 350° for 15 - 20 min. until set.

Cool and cut in squares and put on
cookie sheet to freeze. When frozen
put in freezer bags.

This is one of our favourites for family
fun or formal functions!

Olive Cheese Balls

24 small stuffed olives
1/4 c. butter softened
1 c. or 4 oz. sharp cheddar cheese grated
1/2 c. all purpose flour
1/4 tsp. salt
1/2 tsp. paprika

In small bowl, blend together butter and cheese. Stir in flour, salt and paprika and mix well.

Dry olives on paper towel. Mold dough around olives covering completely.

Bake 400° for 10 min. or until golden.

May be frozen and reheated in foil at 325° for 5 min. These may also be frozen before baking and kept up to 2 months.

For a variation, this dough may be molded around a date, pecan or dill pickle or add 1/4 c. salad olives to the dough and form into small balls, sprinkle with paprika and bake.

Mini Pizza

2 8 oz. cans refrigerated butterflake
   rolls
1 jar or can thick spaghetti sauce,
   chopped olives, mushrooms or whatever
   parmesan or mozarella cheese

Separate each roll in two and flatten
on cookie sheet. Bake for 5 min. - 350°.

Remove and make indent with back of spoon.

Spoon on sauce and topping of your choice.

Top with cheese and bake 350°, 10 - 15
min. or until cheese bubbles.

These can be cooled and frozen.

Mini Quiches

2 pkgs. refrigerator butterflake dinner
  rolls (10 to a pkg.)
1 can sliced mushrooms drained
1 egg beaten
1/2 c. commercial sour cream
1 tbsp. sherry
1/2 tsp. salt
dash of pepper
Gruyère or Swiss cheese

Spray or grease small muffin tins.
Separate each biscuit into two and press
into tins. Place small amount of
mushrooms in each.

Combine egg, sour cream and seasonings
and pour a spoonful on top of the
mushrooms. Cut cheese in small pieces
and place on top.

Bake at 350° for 10 – 15 min.

Cool and freeze.

To reheat, wrap in foil and bake at
300° for 10 min. This makes 40
appeteasers.

Variation

Instead of mushrooms, use small shrimp
(1 can shrimp drained or 1 can flaked
crabmeat).

Or

Get together with a friend and exchange.

19

Old Fashioned
Strips

n sliced bread.

lightly and spread with
e.

is with slightly beaten egg white.

Cut .con in small strips and place on top.

Bake 400° until bacon is cooked.

Cut in quarters and serve hot.

Mother used to make these for Bridge Club and as kids we hoped for left-overs to eat cold for breakfast.

Another Oldie But Goodie

Spread condensed cream of mushroom soup on bread slices (crusts removed).

Roll like jelly roll.

Secure with toothpick and bake 350° until bread is toasted.

These could be cut in half for a nibble or left whole for a snack.

Mushroom Caps

20 large mushrooms
2 medium sized onions
4 oz. cream cheese softened
   Italian dressing mix (the dry kind)
   Accent
   Cayenne

Chop mushroom stems and onions fine,
and sauté in butter until transparent.

Mix with softened cream cheese and fill
mushroom caps.

Sprinkle with Italian dressing mix, a
touch of accent, and a dash of cayenne.

Bake 350° for 10 min. then broil until
slightly brown.

Delicious and different – easily eaten
with the fingers.

21

Stuffed Mushroom Caps

1/2 c. butter
1 tbsp. garlic powder
1 tsp. lemon juice
1 1/2 c. parmesan cheese (approx.)

Melt butter.

Add garlic powder, lemon juice and parmesan cheese.

You may add finely chopped mushroom stems, or 1/2 c. dry bread crumbs at this point if desired.

Fill mushroom caps and place in baking dish.

Bake 350° for 10 min., then broil til nicely browned.

Variation

Before baking, top with an escargot and baste with the melted butter in your pan.

Party Toasted Cheese Squares

1 lb. cheddar cheese grated (2 cups)
1/2 lb. butter softened
1 tsp. dry mustard
1 tsp. worcestershire sauce
1 egg well beaten
1 tbsp. grated onion
1/4 tsp. pepper
2-3 drops tabasco
1 loaf sandwich bread (thinly sliced)

Mix all ingredients except the bread and beat well.

Trim crusts from bread. Using two slices of bread, spread mixture between slices, on top and sides.

Cut sandwiches into 4 squares.

Place in refrigerator for several hours before baking.

Bake on lightly buttered pan for 15 min. at 325° until lightly browned.

Remove and serve hot.

Or, cool on pan and freeze in freezer bags for later use.

If you are a cheese freak like we are, you'll always have a bag of these in your freezer! Bring them out to serve with lunch, for your cocktail hour, or your bed-time snack.

Quick Snack

1/4 lb. butter
1/4 lb. Velveeta cheese
1 c. flour
1/2 tsp. salt
1 tin flakes of ham or 2 tins devilled
   ham

Cream butter and cheese together.

Add flour and salt and mix well.

Pack in 8" square pan.

Spread with ham.

Heat oven to 450°. Turn off heat when these go in oven and leave until ready to serve. (Leave at least 45 min.)

These can be made in a hurry and then just left in oven until ready to serve.

Delicious! So easy, even our friend Gracious can make these!

Roast Pig Tails

10 lb. box short pig tails
1 10 oz. can beef gravy or freeze left
    over gravy from beef, chicken or
    turkey and save for this recipe
5 c. boiling water
3 tbsp. vinegar
6 tbsp. brown sugar
1 tsp. salt
1 tsp. accent
1/2 tsp. pepper
1 tsp. garlic salt
3 tbsp. gravey improver

Trim fat from pig tails.

Mix all ingredients.

Put pig tails in large roasting pan and
pour sauce over.

Bake uncovered at 325° for 3 hours.

Baste every 20 min. During last hour
of baking, pour in a bottle of beer.
This will cut the fat.

A traditional Waterloo County meal
served with sauerkraut (with caraway)
or as a nifty nibble.

Sausage and Bacon Quiche

3 c. chopped onion
1 lb. sausage meat
1/2 lb. bacon, cut in fine pieces
1 1/2 c. commercial sour cream
2 tbsp. flour
1/3 c. milk
1/2 tsp. salt
3 eggs beaten
1 tsp. caraway seeds
1 pkg. refrigerator crescent rolls

Brown onions and bacon pieces. Drain off grease and set aside on paper towels.

Brown sausage meat and drain well.

Blend sour cream with flour and stir in milk, salt, beaten eggs and caraway seeds.

Unroll crescent rolls and press in 9 X 15 pan covering bottom and up sides.

Spread bacon, onion and sausage mixture over dough.

Pour sour cream mixture on top.

Bake 325° for 40 min. or until filling is set. Cut into snack pieces and serve hot.

May be frozen. Put pieces on cookie sheet in freezer and when frozen, put in plastic bag.

This is also good with coffee for brunch. Serve with Grandma Prange's tomato butter.

Savoury Snacks

1/2 lb. ground lean beef
1/4 c. chopped onion
1 c. chopped celery
1 envelope Sloppy Joe mix (dry)
1 can (5 1/2 oz.) tomato paste
3/4 c. water
2 tbsp. apple jelly or red currant jelly
1 pkg. refrigerator butterflake rolls (10)

Brown meat and onions. Add all other ingredients.

Divide each butterflake roll into two and press into small muffin tins. Put filling in and bake 350° for 15 min.

Cool and freeze.

For cheese lovers, top with your favourite cheese before baking.

This filling can be made ahead and put in jars and stored in the refrigerator.

27

Scotch Eggs

6 hard boiled eggs, shelled
1 lb. sausage meat
2 eggs beaten
salt and pepper to taste
1/4 tsp. sage
1/4 tsp. basil (optional)
1/4 c. flour
cracker crumbs
oil for browning

Cut sausage into 6 equal slices. Flour hands and place a slice of sausage in palm. Place an egg in centre and work meat around.

Dip in flour, raw egg and crumbs. Fry on all sides in 1" hot oil.

Slice and serve hot as a finger food or serve whole with potato salad for lunch.

Turn this one into breakfast for guests but don't forget the tomato butter!

28

Water Chestnuts Wrapped In Bacon

1/4 c. oil
1/4 c. soya sauce
2 tbsp. ketchup
1 tbsp. vinegar
dash pepper
2 cloves garlic crushed
2 cans water chestnuts drained
1 lb. bacon cut in half slices

Mix all ingredients except chestnuts and bacon.

Add chestnuts to sauce and marinate 4 hrs.

Wrap each chestnut in half slice of bacon and secure with toothpick.

Broil at 500° for 8 - 10 min. or until bacon is done. Serve hot.

Or cool and put in plastic bags and freeze for later use.

Variation.

1. Marinate chicken livers in sauce for 4 hrs. and wrap with bacon and broil.

2. Sprinkle smoked oysters with lemon juice and wrap bacon half around two smoked oysters and broil.

Wilma's Glazed Sausage Bites

1 lb. bulk pork sausage
1 slightly beaten egg
1/2 c. cracker crumbs
1/2 tsp. sage

Combine above. Shape into 1" balls and brown slowly. Don't brown in oil as these are quite gooey.

Sauce

1/4 c. water
1/4 c. ketchup
2 tbsp. brown sugar
1 tbsp. vinegar
1 tbsp. soya sauce

Combine sauce ingredients and pour over sausage balls. Simmer 15 min. Stir occasionally. Serve with cocktail picks or forks.

Your men folk could make a meal of these, so make it for dinner with rice!

SAY CHEESE!

Dried Beef Log

1 8 oz. cream cheese softened
1 tbsp. grated onion or onion flakes
1/4 c. parmesan cheese
1 tbsp. horseradish sauce
1 2 1/2 oz. chipped beef

Blend together all except beef. Put in refrigerator to harden.

Chop dried beef finely.

Shape cheese in log and roll in chipped beef.

If you can't find chipped beef, just as good rolled in flaked corned beef.

Ham and Pineapple Log

1 8 oz. cream cheese
1 small tin crushed pineapple well drained
   on paper towels
1 c. chopped pecans
1/4 c. chopped green peppers
1 tbsp. finely chopped onion
1 1/2 tsp. seasoned salt
1 small can devilled (4 oz.) ham

Mix all but nuts.

Refrigerate to harden.

Roll in pecans.

Freezer Cheese Balls

8 oz. sharp cheddar cheese
1 clove garlic minced
1 8 oz. pkg. cream cheese
4 oz. blue cheese
1/4 c. butter
3/4 c. chopped nuts, walnuts or pecans

Shred the cheddar cheese.

Soften cream cheese.

Mix cheeses together with blue cheese.

Mix in garlic and butter.

Chill well and form into 4 balls and
roll in chopped nuts.

May be frozen.

Ham and Cheese Ball

1   8 oz. pkg. cream cheese
1/4 c. mayonnaise
2   8 oz. tins flakes of ham
2 tbsp. chopped parsley or 3 tbsp.
    chopped salad olives or both
1 tsp. minced onion
1/4 tsp. dry mustard
1/4 tsp. tabasco
1/2 c. chopped nuts

Cream the cheese and mayonnaise until smooth. Stir in the next 5 ingredients.

Cover and chill several hours.

Mold into two balls and roll in chopped nuts.

This may also be frozen.

Nippy Corned Beef & Cheese Ball

1 small pkg. cream cheese softened
1 c. grated cheddar cheese
1 can (6 oz.) corned beef, shredded
1 tsp. horseradish.
1 tsp. prepared mustard
1/4 tsp. worcestershire sauce
1/4 tsp. grated lemon rind
2 tbsp. lemon juice
1/3 c. sweet pickle relish, drained
1/2 c. parsley flakes·

In a mixer bowl (or food processor) blend together thoroughly: cheeses, corned beef, horseradish, mustard, worcestershire sauce, lemon rind and juice and pickle relish.

Cover and refrigerate until firm.

Shape into two balls and roll in parsley.

Wrap and refrigerate or freeze.

34

Party Cheese Ball

1 lb. sharp cheddar cheese, grated
2 8 oz. pkgs. cream cheese softened
1/2 c. chopped stuffed olives
1/4 tsp. baking soda
1/4 c. evaporated milk
1/2 tsp. tabasco sauce
1 tbsp. parsley flakes
1 tbsp. grated onion or onion flakes
1 clove garlic minced or 1 tsp. garlic
  powder
1 tbsp. worcestershire sauce
1 tsp. lemon juice
1 c. chopped pecans

Combine cheeses and mix well. Add remaining ingredients except chopped pecans.

Refrigerate for 2 - 3 hrs.

Mold into two balls or two logs and roll in chopped nuts or add chopped pecans with the rest of ingredients and mold into two balls.

This will freeze.

Pineapple Cheese Balls

3 oz. pkg. cream cheese
1/4 c. drained, crushed pineapple
1/4 c. chopped nuts

Cream cheese until smooth.

Add pineapple and blend.

Form into 1/2" balls and roll in chopped nuts.

Chill. At serving time, pierce each ball with a pretzel stick.

Yield - 24 balls.

Pop's Potted Cheese

1 lb. old cheddar cheese grated
1/4 c. minced green onion tops
1 tbsp. Dijon mustard
1 oz. cognac, brandy or dry sherry
2 tbsp. butter softened
    (cream optional)

Combine cheese and onion tops.

Gradually blend in mustard, cognac and butter.

Stir until smooth, adding more butter or cream to make it easy to spread.

Pack into small crocks and seal tightly with plastic wrap and store in refrigerator.

Serve at room temperature.

This is delicious on French bread or crackers with a soup or salad supper!

If you like curry, 1/2 tsp. curry powder added to this, gives a nice flavour.

This improves with age - like Pop!

Sir Sam's Wheel of Brie

1 tin of Brie Cheese
2 tbsp. butter
1 tbsp. lemon juice
1 tsp. garlic powder
2 tbsp. unblanched almonds
   Pumpernickel Bread

Remove foil from cheese and place on oven-proof plate.

In small saucepan, melt butter, add lemon juice and garlic powder and stir.

Spoon butter mixture over cheese and put almonds on top.

Bake at 300° for 20 min. until almonds are brown and cheese is heated through.

Remove to round platter and cut Pumpernickel Bread into triangles and arrange around cheese to look like spokes of a wheel.

This is also good using camembert and nuts of your choice.

We shared this as an appetizer before dinner on a ski week-end at Sir Sam's in Haliburton. The chef was kind enough to give us his recipe. We found it _too_ delicious to share.

Three Cheese Ball

4 oz. smoked cheese
4 oz. blue cheese
8 oz. cream cheese
1 tsp. worcestershire sauce
1 tbsp. onion flakes
2 tbsp. minced parsley
1/2 c. chopped pecans

Beat cheese until fluffy.

Beat in onion and worcestershire sauce.

Cover and chill in refrigerator overnight.

Mold mixture into one large or two smaller balls and roll in nut and parsley mixture.

May be frozen.

Serve as spread with variety of crackers.

DIPS AND SPREADS

Blue Cheese Dip

1 c. mayonnaise
2 tbsp. finely chopped onion
1 tbsp. garlic powder
1/4 c. finely chopped parsley
1/2 c. sour cream
1 tbsp. lemon juice
1 tbsp. white vinegar
1/4 c. blue cheese crumbled
   salt if desired
   freshly ground pepper
   dash cayenne

Combine all ingredients in a mixing bowl.

Refrigerate for at least 1 hr. Yields 2 1/2 cups.

Garlic Butter

1/2 lb. butter (room temperature)
2 tbsp. chopped parsley
4-5 garlic cloves minced
   fresh pepper
1 tbsp. onion flakes
1/2 tbsp. lemon juice

Mix all ingredients.

To store, roll in aluminum foil.

Will keep in refrigerator for 3 months.

A good make-ahead if you're serving garlic bread instead of our lunch muffins!

41

Canapé Spreads

A

1 8 oz. pkg. cream cheese softened
1/2 c. mayonnaise
1/2 c. finely chopped walnuts
1 small can crushed pineapple, drained

Blend all ingredients and chill.

B

2 c. ground ham or flakes of ham
1/2 c. mayonnaise
2 hard cooked eggs, chopped
1/4 c. ground sweet pickles or drained
       pickle relish
2 tbsp. finely chopped onion

Blend all ingredients and chill.

C

8 oz. cottage cheese
1 can flakes of chicken
3 tbsp. finely chopped onion
2 tbsp. parsley flakes
1/4 tsp. garlic powder
1/4 tsp. paprika

Blend all ingredients together in blender
and chill.

Easy, make-ahead spreads for crunchy
veggies and crackers.

Donna's Antipasto

1/2 small head cauliflower separated
    into tiny flowerettes
1 8 oz. jar olives with pimento (drained)
1 8 oz. jar sweet pickled onions (drained)
32 oz. bottle ketchup
3 green peppers chopped
1/2 c. olive or corn oil
1/4 c. vinegar
2 cans (7 oz.) chunk tuna, drained
1 can sliced mushrooms, drained
1 can (7 oz.) small shrimp, drained
1 14 oz. jar pitted black olives, sliced
    (optional) — we leave out

In large saucepan pre-cook cauliflowerettes
5 min. and drain. Add olives, onions,
ketchup, peppers, oil and vinegar and
simmer gently 10 min.

Add tuna, mushrooms and shrimp. Simmer
gently for 30 min.

Bottle and refrigerate.

This makes about 2 quarts and keeps for
ages.

Serve with rye bread or melba toast and
crackers.

Simply scrumptious.

This takes a little more time, but makes
a large quantity and is well worth the
effort.

Frosted Liver Pâté

1 lb. liverwurst
3 tbsp. minced onion
1 clove garlic, crushed
1/2 tsp. basil, thyme and oregano

Mash liverwurst and mix in all other
ingredients. Place on plate and shape
into loaf with rounded top. Chill.

Ice with cream cheese topping:

1 8 oz. pkg. cream cheese softened
1 tsp. mayonnaise
1 clove garlic minced
dash tabasco

Mix all ingredients together and ice pâté.
This may be decorated for party fun with
parsley, etc.

Try shaping into a football for a Grey
Cup party and make stripes with red
pimento.

Glazed Braunschweiger Mousse

1 envelope unflavoured gelatin
1 10 oz. tin consommé
1/2 lb. or 1 roll braunschweiger
3 tbsp. mayonnaise
1/2 onion, chopped fine
1 tsp. worcestershire sauce
1 tsp. vinegar
dash pepper

Soften gelatin in 1/4 c. cold water.

Heat consommé to boiling and add softened gelatin.

Put a thin layer in bottom of mold or individual molds. Chill.

Blend all other ingredients thoroughly.

Fill mold or molds with meat mixture and pour rest of consommé over.

Chill until firm.

Unmold and serve with rye bread and crackers. May be frozen.

For a nice change, try adding some brandy, sherry, nuts or olives to the meat mixture.

Grandma Prange's Tomato Butter

1 6 qt. basket ripe tomatoes
4 c. vinegar
1 small bag pickling spice
1 red sweet pepper, cut fine
1 1/2 tbsp. salt
3 lbs. (6 cups) white sugar

Skin and slice tomatoes and let stand over night.

Drain off water.

To pulp, add the vinegar and boil until soft.

Add bag of pickling spice and the red pepper and salt.

Boil 1 hr. then add 3 lbs. (6 cups) white sugar and boil until thick, at least 3 hrs.

Stir often to prevent burning.

Pour into sterilized jars. Makes about 4 - 6 pts.

A very old recipe and super with bacon and eggs and all meats for dinner. We love to put it on a slice of tomato.

Homemade Mayonnaise

3/4 c. white sugar
1 1/2 tsp. salt
1 1/2 tsp. cornstarch
2 tsp. mustard
3/4 c. vinegar
2 eggs
1 tbsp. butter

Mix sugar, salt, cornstarch and mustard together.

Gradually add vinegar and bring to a boil.

Beat eggs, add small amount of hot mixture to eggs first and then add all the egg mixture to the hot mixture and boil again until thickened.

Remove from heat and add butter. Pour in jar.

A sweet mayonnaise for sandwich fillings and devilled eggs.

Mildred's Chicken Liver Pâté

1 c. butter
1 lb. chicken livers
1 medium onion sliced
1/2 tsp. curry powder
1/2 tsp. paprika
1/4 tsp. salt
1/8 tsp. pepper
1-2 cloves garlic, crushed

Trim fat off chicken livers if any.

Melt the butter and cook the chicken livers, onion, and seasonings in butter over medium heat until onions are soft.

Blend in blender or food processor, a small amount at a time until smooth.

Pour in mold or loaf pan and chill overnight. Serve with triscuits or melba toast.

Even our non-liver-lover friends enjoyed this tasty and simple recipe.

Mrs. Scott's Mustard

1 c. brown sugar
1/3 c. dry mustard
2 eggs
1/3 c. cider vinegar
2 tbsp. butter

Mix together the brown sugar, dry mustard, eggs, and vinegar. Cook until thick.

Remove from heat and add the butter.

Store in jar.

This is a yummy sweet mustard – not too hot. Good as a dip for cocktail sausages or sausage balls. A must at Octoberfest with ham and roast pork.

Mrs. Scott's Seafood Sauce

2 oz. malt vinegar
1/8 tsp. salt
1/2 tsp. worcestershire sauce
1/2 tsp. tabasco
2 oz. horseradish
3 oz. chili sauce
3 oz. ketchup

Mix together. For shrimp cocktail, add shrimp, let stand in refrigerator an hour or more.

OR

Serve as a dip for shrimp.

Quick & Easy Vegetable Dips

A

1 pkg. dry Italian Salad Dressing Mix
1 pint commercial sour cream
1/4 tsp. curry powder

Simply stir together and store in refrigerator.

B

1 c. mayonnaise
1/2 c. sour cream
1 clove garlic crushed
1 small onion chopped fine
1 green onion chopped fine
dash of salt, celery salt, garlic salt
    and worcestershire sauce

Mix all ingredients well.

Adjust seasonings to your own taste.

Store in jar in refrigerator.

Sweet and Sour Sauce

3/4 c. brown sugar
1/4 c. soya sauce
1/3 c. vinegar
2/3 c. water
2 tbsp. ketchup
3 tbsp. cornstarch dissolved in 1/4 c. water

Bring this to a boil.

Store in refrigerator for future use.

Heat to serve as a dip with our sausage balls, or spoon over a meat loaf before baking. A hit with your kids!

Barbecue Sauce

1 tin tomato soup
1/2 c. brown sugar
1/2 c. vinegar
1/2 tsp. paprika
1 tsp. celery salt
1 tsp. chili powder
1/2 tsp. ground cloves
dash salt

Stir together all ingredients and heat.

An excellent sauce for ribs, tails, chicken, chops, etc.

Toppings for Cream Cheese

A

1 8 oz. jar pineapple jam
1 8 oz. jar apple jelly
1 tbsp. dry mustard
2 1/2 oz. horseradish

Just mix together and store in the same jars in refrigerator. May be kept for months.

Spoon over a bar of cream cheese and serve with crackers.

B

Place an 8 oz. bar of cream cheese in small serving dish. Prick with a fork.

Marinate in 1 tbsp. soya sauce for a few hours.

Delicious spread on melba toast or crackers.

May also be sprinkled with toasted almonds or toasted sesame seeds.

Dips for Fruit

Chocolate Dip

Pour 3 oz. whipping cream in saucepan.

Add 3 squares semi-sweet chocolate and stir until creamy at low heat.

Add 2 tsp. Grand Marnier.

For dipping bananas, maraschino cherries with stems, apples, or pears.

Crème Fraîche

1 c. whipping cream
1/2 c. sour cream
    grated peel of 1 lemon
4 tsp. lemon juice
2 tsp. granulated sugar

In small bowl, mix whipping cream and sour cream until smooth.

Cover and let stand at room temperature until thick (about 24 hrs.).

Stir in lemon peel, lemon juice and sugar.

Cover and refrigerate. Will keep for at least 3 days. Makes 1 1/2 cups.

53

Dips for Fruit

Cream Cheese Dip

Soften an 8 oz. bar cream cheese

Add 1 c. frozen strawberries (slightly thawed).

Put in blender and blend until smooth.

Add more strawberries for a pinker colour if desired.

A little sugar may be added for a sweeter taste.

Delicious for bananas, pineapple, apple, grapes or all fresh fruit.

Sour Cream Dip

Mix 1 c. dairy sour cream with 2 tbsp. of dark brown sugar.

Spoon into bowl and sprinkle with small amount of brown sugar.

HOOKED ON SEAFOOD

Crabmeat Appetizers

1 can refrigerated butterflake biscuits
   (10 in can)
1 7 oz. can crab meat, drained and
      flaked
1/4 c. minced celery
1/2 tsp. salt
1/2 tsp. dry mustard
      dash tabasco
      dash worcestershire
1/4 c. commercial sour cream
2 tbsp. mayonnaise
1/4 c. shredded cheddar cheese (or more)

Divide each biscuit in half. Press into small muffin cups.

Meanwhile, mix all remaining ingredients except cheese.

Place about one tablespoon of filling in each shell. Top with a sprinkle of cheese.

Bake 350° for 15 min. or until cheese is melted.

Cool and freeze.

Makes 20 appetizers.

Crab Swiss Bites

1 can crab meat, drained and flaked
1 c. Swiss cheese grated (4 oz.)
1/2 c. mayonnaise
1 tbsp. chopped onion
1 tsp. lemon juice
1/2 tsp. salt
1/4 tsp. curry powder
1 pkg. refrigerator butterflake rolls

Combine all ingredients except rolls.

Separate rolls in three and place on ungreased cookie sheet.

Spoon crab mixture on biscuits.

Bake 350° for 10 min.

Try putting a slice of water chestnut on top of crab mixture before baking.

Donna's Shrimp Mousse

1 envelope unflavoured gelatin
1/4 c. cold water
1 8 oz. pkg. cream cheese
1 10 oz. can tomato soup
1 c. mayonnaise
2 cans small shrimp drained and cut into
    pieces
1/2 c. onion, chopped fine
1 green pepper, chopped fine

Soften gelatin in cold water.

Put cream cheese and soup in double
boiler and heat and stir until well
blended. (Beat with beaters if it isn't
smooth enough.)

Stir gelatin and mayonnaise into soup
mixture.

Let cool slightly, then stir in shrimp,
onion and green pepper.

Pour into oiled 4 cup mold or individual
molds and chill.

Unmold and garnish with parsley and
shrimp. Serve with assorted crackers.

May be stored in refrigerator for a couple
of days or may be frozen.

Hot Crab and Cheese Dip

1   8 oz. pkg. cream cheese
1   7 oz. can flaked crab meat
    Worcestershire sauce to taste (1/2 -
    1 tsp.)
    Tabasco sauce to taste (couple of
    drops)
1 tbsp. sour cream
1 tbsp. lemon juice or white vinegar
1/4 tsp. salt
grated parmesan cheese

Mix all ingredients except parmesan
cheese together.

Sprinkle parmesan on top.

Put in oven-proof dish, one that may be
taken to the table, and bake at 350° for
1/2 hr.

Ready for cracker dipping.

For those who can't eat sea food,
substitute flakes of ham or corned beef
for the crab - just as good!

Louise's Crab Stuffed Snow Peas

1/3 lb. fresh snow peas (30 - 36 peas)
1   7 oz. can crab meat, drained
1 tbsp. mayonnaise
    salt and pepper
1 tbsp. chili sauce or sea food sauce
    dash tabasco

Steam peas for 1 min., no longer as they should be a bright green.

Drain in cold water.

Mix the rest of the ingredients together.

Carefully open pods and stuff with crab mixture.

Chill.

Variation:

Stuff with 4 oz. softened cream cheese, mixed with 1 tbsp. parsley, 1/2 tsp. dried basil, and 1 tsp. lemon juice.

A gourmet treat for crab lovers, and an attractive addition to your nibble tray.

Pat Scott's Lobster Roll

1/2 lb. velveeta cheese
1/4 lb. butter
2 6 oz. cans lobster or crab, drained
1 large loaf sliced bread

Melt butter and cheese and add lobster
or crab.

Trim crusts from bread, roll thin and
spread each slice with mixture.

Roll, wrap in foil and freeze.

To serve, slice rolls in half rounds,
dip in melted butter, bake on cookie
sheet 10 - 12 min. in 350° oven.

Makes 40 snacks.

Dee's Crab Meat Appetizers

1 pkg. frozen cocktail vol-au-vent
        (patti shells)
1 can crab meat
1 scant cup processed cheese
1 tsp. worcestershire sauce
1/4 tsp. pepper
1/2 tsp. onion powder
1 egg yolk

Combine ingredients and fill shells.
Freeze. When ready to use, bake
10 min. at 400°.

Salmon Dip

4 oz. cream cheese softened
1 c. commercial sour cream
2 tbsp. mayonnaise
1 tsp. lemon juice
1/2 tsp. grated lemon peel
2 tbsp. finely chopped celery
2 tbsp. finely chopped green onion
1 can (7 3/4 oz.) salmon, drained
salt and freshly ground pepper

Blend together cream cheese, sour cream, mayonnaise, lemon juice and peel.

Stir in remaining ingredients, seasoning to taste with salt and pepper.

Chill.

Makes about 2 cups.

Shrimp Dip

3/4 c. small shrimp drained
1/2 c. chili sauce
3 tbsp. tomato paste
2 tbsp. lemon juice
8 oz. cream cheese
1 tbsp. horseradish
1/4 c. chopped dill pickles

Mix ingredients together.

Makes 2 cups.

May be frozen.

Tastes like a shrimp cocktail when served with crackers.

61

Salmon Log

1   16 oz. can red salmon
1   8 oz. pkg. cream cheese softened
1   tbsp. lemon juice
2   tsp. grated onion
1   tsp. prepared horseradish
1/4 tsp. liquid smoke
3   tbsp. chopped parsley or parsley flakes
1/2 c. chopped pecans

Drain and flake salmon, removing skin and bones.

Combine all other ingredients except nuts and parsley.

Chill several hours.

Mix chopped pecans and parsley. Shape salmon mixture into log and roll in parsley-nut mixture and refrigerate.

May be frozen.

It is hard to find liquid smoke but we can usually find it in a cheese specialty store. Share the bottle with friends as a little goes a long way.

Salmon Mousse

1 tbsp. gelatin
1/4 c. cold water — include liquid from
   salmon
1/2 c. chopped celery or green pepper
3/4 c. salad dressing or mayonnaise
1 7 3/4 oz. tin salmon
1/4 c. chopped olives
1 tbsp. lemon juice
season to taste

Sprinkle gelatin over cold water, and
place over low heat until dissolved.

Add to dressing.

Fold in salmon, celery, olives and
seasoning.

Place in small individual molds for
your hors d'oeuvres tray, or in your
sea food mold for your buffet table.

Sardine Pâté

2 3 1/2 oz. cans sardines
6 tbsp. butter
2 tbsp. cream cheese
1 tbsp. lemon juice
1 tbsp. worcestershire sauce
1 tsp. ketchup
  dash garlic powder
1/4 tsp. salt
1/8 tsp. cayenne

Mash sardines. Mix with the butter
and cheese and blend to a smooth paste.

Season with lemon juice, worcestershire,
ketchup, garlic, salt and cayenne.

Refrigerate. Makes 1 cup.

Tuna Cups

1 small can tuna
1 hard cooked egg chopped
1 c. (4 oz.) shredded cheddar cheese
1/3 c. chopped celery
1/4 c. mayonnaise
1 8 oz. can refrigerated butterflake rolls

Combine tuna, egg, cheese, celery and
mayonnaise. Mix well.

Separate butterflake rolls and divide
each one in two. Press into ungreased
muffin cups around and up the sides.

Spoon tuna mixture into cups.

Bake 10 - 15 min. at 350°. Makes 20.

Our tasters thought these were delicious
and a nice change from the richness of
shell fish.

Metric Conversion

Spoons

	Rounded
1/4 teaspoon	1 ml
1/2 teaspoon	2 ml
1 teaspoon	5 ml
2 teaspoons	10 ml
1 tablespoon	15 ml

Cups

1/4 cup	50 ml
1/3 cup	75 ml
1/2 cup	125 ml
2/3 cup	150 ml
3/4 cup	175 ml
1 cup	250 ml

Ounces

1 oz.	30 grams
2 oz.	55 grams
3 oz.	85 grams
4 oz.	115 grams
5 oz.	140 grams
6 oz.	170 grams
7 oz.	200 grams
8 oz.	250 grams
16 oz.	500 grams
32 oz.	1,000 grams, 1 kg

A Great Idea For:

> Showers, bridge prizes, stocking stuffers, host or hostess gift, or just an inexpensive gift for cooks of all ages.

Please send me:

_____ copies of Muffin Mania
at $6.95 per copy

_____ copies of La Manie des Muffins
at $6.95 per copy

_____ copies of Nibble Mania
at $6.95 per copy

_____ copies of Veggie Mania
at $6.95 per copy

_____ copies of Sweet Mania
at $6.95 per copy

Plus $2.00 per copy for mailing, handling, and G.S.T.

Enclosed is $_____

Name _____

Street _____

City _____

Province _____ Postal Code _____

Make cheque payable to:

> Muffin Mania Publishing Co.,
> c/o Mrs. Cathy Prange,
> 184 Lydia St.,
> Kitchener, Ont. N2H 1W1

notes

notes

Notes